First World War
and Army of Occupation
War Diary
France, Belgium and Germany

9 DIVISION
1 Lowland Brigades
Highland Light Infantry
51st (Grad.) Battalion.
18 March 1919 - 30 September 1919

WO95/1776/3

The Naval & Military Press Ltd
www.nmarchive.com
Published in association with The National Archives

Published by

The Naval & Military Press Ltd

Unit 10 Ridgewood Industrial Park,

Uckfield, East Sussex,

TN22 5QE England

Tel: +44 (0) 1825 749494

www.naval-military-press.com

www.nmarchive.com

This diary has been reprinted in facsimile from the original. Any imperfections are inevitably reproduced and the quality may fall short of modern type and cartographic standards.

© **Crown Copyright**
Images reproduced by permission of The National Archives, London, England, 2015.

Contents

Document type	Place/Title	Date From	Date To
Heading	Lowland Late 9th Division 1 Lowland Bde 51th H.L.I 1919 Mar-1919 Sep From U.K		
Heading	51st Bn Highland Light Infantry War Diary From 18/3/1919 To 31/3/1919		
War Diary	Dunkirk	18/03/1919	20/03/1919
War Diary	Solingen	21/03/1919	31/03/1919
Heading	War Diary of 51st Bn Highland Light Infantry For Month Of April 1919		
War Diary	Solingen	01/04/1919	28/04/1919
Heading	War Diary 51st Bn Highland Light Infantry For Month Of May 1919		
War Diary	Solingen	30/04/1919	31/05/1919
Heading	War Diary 51st Bn Highland Light Infantry For Month Of June 1919		
War Diary	Solingen	01/06/1919	30/06/1919
Heading	War Diary 51st Bn The Highland Light Infantry Month Of September 1919		
War Diary	Stommeln	01/09/1919	27/09/1919
War Diary	Bedburg	28/09/1919	30/09/1919
Heading	War Diary 51st Bn. The Highland Light Infantry For Month Of August 1919		
War Diary	Worringen	01/08/1919	07/08/1919
War Diary	Stommeln	08/08/1919	31/08/1919
Heading	War Diary 51st Bn. The Highland Light Infantry Month Of September 1919		
War Diary	Stommeln	01/09/1919	26/09/1919
War Diary	Bedburg	27/09/1919	30/09/1919

LOWLAND LATE: 9ᵗʰ DIVISION

1 LOWLAND BDE

51ˢᵗ H L S

1919 MAR – 1919 SEP

from UK

51st Bn. Highland Light Infantry

War Diary

From 18/3/1919 to 31/3/1919

W.H. Green Capt & Adjt
for Major
Commanding 51st Bn High. L. Infy.

Army Form C. 2118.

WAR DIARY
or
INTELLIGENCE SUMMARY

(Erase heading not required.)

Instructions regarding War Diaries and Intelligence Summaries are contained in F. S. Regs., Part II. and the Staff Manual respectively. Title Pages will be prepared in manuscript.

Place	Date	Hour	Summary of Events and Information	Remarks and references to Appendices
Dunkirk	18/3/19		Battalion arrives Dunkirk from England	
	19/3/19		Departure from Dunkirk for Solesmes	
	20/3/19		Journey occupies two days.	
	21/3/19		Battalion arrives Solesmes	
	22/3/19		Companies at disposal of Coy. Commanders for Interior Economy	
	23/3/19		Church Parade	
Solesmes	24/3/19		Training as per programme.	
	25/3/19		Do Do	
	26/3/19		Do Do	
	27/3/19		Do Do	
	28/3/19		Bath. for A. B. & C Coys.	
	29/3/19		Do D Coy. & No. 2 Coy	
	30/3/19		Church Parade.	
	31/3/19		Training as per programme	

2449 Wt. W14957/M90 750,000 1/16 J.B.C. & A. Forms/C.2118/12.

WAR DIARY

of

51st. Bn. Highland Light Infantry.

for

Month of April 1919.

[signature]
Lieut. Col.
Commanding 51st. High. L.I.

Army Form C. 2118.

WAR DIARY
or
INTELLIGENCE SUMMARY

(Erase heading not required.)

Place	Date	Hour	Summary of Events and Information	Remarks and references to Appendices
Solingen	1/4/19	—	Training as per programme.	
do	2/4/19	—	do.	
do	3/4/19	09.30 / 6.400 / 14.30	Baths for "C" Coy, Transport & Headquarters. Lecture by Professor Aitkins "The Balkan Tangle" Training as per programme. Baths for "D" Coy.	
do	4/4/19		do.	
do	5/4/19		do.	
do	6/4/19	09.00	Church Parade.	
do	7/4/19		Training as per programme. — 2 Platoons on Wiring Outpost Line	
do	8/4/19		Education and training as per programme. do. do.	
do	9/4/19		do. do. do.	
do	10/4/19		do. do. do.	
do	11/4/19	09.30 / 6.14.00 / 17.00	Baths for "B" Coy, Transport, H.Q.Coy, & Canals do. do. Lecture by Rev. C.H. Hazlett B.A. "Danger & Prevention of Venereal Disease" do. do. Training as per programme. Baths for "C" Coy	
do	12/4/19		Church Parade.	
do	13/4/19	09.00	Training as per programme. "B" Coy relieved "B" Coy on Outpost Line	
do	14/4/19		do. do. "L" Coy " "A" Coy " "	
do	15/4/19		do. do. 2 Platoons wiring	
do	16/4/19		do. do.	
do	17/4/19		do. do.	
do	18/4/19	09.00 / 6.14.30	Baths for "A" Coy, Transports, H.Q.Coy & Canals. N.Co. with A & B Coy. 2 Platoons wiring Divisional Sa. 2 Platoons wiring "Good Friday"	

Sheet No. 2.

Army Form C. 2118.

WAR DIARY
or
INTELLIGENCE SUMMARY
(Erase heading not required.)

Instructions regarding War Diaries and Intelligence Summaries are contained in F.S. Regs., Part II. and the Staff Manual respectively. Title Pages will be prepared in manuscript.

Place	Date	Hour	Summary of Events and Information	Remarks and references to Appendices
Solingen	19/4/19	09.30 h / 11.30	Bath for B Coy. Football match with 3/6 Royal Scots (Infantry)	
do.	20/4/19	09.00 h	Lt. Col. W.H.E. Segrave D.S.O. Command of Battn taken over by. Church Parade	
do	21/4/19		Training as per programme	
do	22/4/19		do	
do	23/4/19		do	
do	24/4/19	14.00 h / 17.00	Baths, Transport HQ Coy & "A" Coy. Wiring Party 2 Platoons wiring	
do	25/4/19	08.30 h / 10.30	Baths for "A" Coy & Canals " do do	
do	26/4/19		Strengthening Outpost Line. "B" Coy takes over. Football match with 18th Bn H.L.I.	
do	27/4/19	14.15 h		
do	28/4/19		Church Parades	
do	29/4/19		Training as per programme	

WAR DIARY.

51st. BN. HIGHLAND LIGHT INFANTRY.

FOR MONTH OF MAY, 1919.

LT. COL.

COMMANDING 51st. BN.HIGH.L.I.

Army Form C. 2118.

WAR DIARY
or
INTELLIGENCE SUMMARY

(Erase heading not required.)

Instructions regarding War Diaries and Intelligence Summaries are contained in F. S. Regs., Part II. and the Staff Manual respectively. Title Pages will be prepared in manuscript.

Place	Date	Hour	Summary of Events and Information	Remarks and references to Appendices
Solingen	30/4/19		Training as per programme.	
	1/5/19		Hockey match with 15th Bn High L.I.	
	2/5/19		Baths for H Coy & Head Quarters Coy. Training as per programme. Baths for Transport & Casuals.	
	3/5/19		Training as per programme.	
	4/5/19		Training as per programme. Football match (Association) A Coy v. Field Ambulance. Church Parade.	
	5/5/19		Training as per programme.	
	6/5/19		A Coy relieved D Coy on Outpost Line. Training as per programme.	
	7/5/19		Inspection by Field Marshall H.R.H. the Duke of Connaught, Colonel-in-Chief, High. L.I.	
	8/5/19		Training as per programme. Baths for Transport & Casuals.	
	9/5/19		Training as for programme. Baths for B Coy & H.Q. Company	

Army Form C. 2118.

WAR DIARY
or
INTELLIGENCE SUMMARY
(Erase heading not required.)

Instructions regarding War Diaries and Intelligence Summaries are contained in F. S. Regs., Part II. and the Staff Manual respectively. Title Pages will be prepared in manuscript.

Place	Date	Hour	Summary of Events and Information	Remarks and references to Appendices
Solingen	10/5/19		Training as per programme.	
	11/5/19		Football (Association) A Coy 51st Bn Mgt. L.I. v Company from 15th Bn Mgt. L.I.	
	12/5/19		Church Parade.	
	13/5/19		Training as per programme.	
	14/5/19		Lecture by Rev. Archdeacon Jones. Subject - "British Channel Burrows."	
	15/5/19		Training as per programme	
			Baths for B Coy. 112 Bay.	
	16/5/19		Training as per programme.	
			Baths for Transport Animals	
	17/5/19		Training as per programme	
	18/5/19		Training as per programme	
			Football A Coy 51st Bn Mgt L.I. v B Coy 5th K.O.S.B. in "Best Company Cup".	
	19/5/19		Church Parade.	
			Hockey match. Officers 51st B.M.C.S. 51st Bn Mgt. L.I. v 1/5th K.O.S.B.	
	20/5/19		Training as per programme.	
	21/5/19		Do Do	

2449 Wt. W14957/M90 750,000 1/16 J.B.C. & A. Forms/C.2118/12.

WAR DIARY
INTELLIGENCE SUMMARY

Army Form C. 2118.

Place	Date	Hour	Summary of Events and Information	Remarks and references to Appendices
Solingen	22/5/19		Baths for D. Coy.	
	23/5/19		Training as per programme. Baths for H.2. Coy. Transport.	
	24/5/19		Training as per programme	
	25/5/19		Do. Do. Church Parade.	
	26/5/19		Training as per programme. Lecture by Lt. Col. Ingham "The Palaces of Peterwein"	
	27/5/19		Training as per programme.	
	28/5/19		Baths for D. Coy. Training as per programme.	
	29/5/19		Baths for Transport. Lecture by M.A.J. Glasspool on "Norway, its Antics, People & Scenery".	
	30/5/19		Training as per programme. Baths for H.2. Coy. Transport.	
	31/5/19		Training as per programme. Do.	

War Diary

51st Bn Highland Light Infantry

For month of June 1919

E Seagrave
Lt. Col.
Commanding 51st Bn High. L.I.

Army Form C. 2118.

WAR DIARY
or
INTELLIGENCE SUMMARY
(Erase heading not required.)

Instructions regarding War Diaries and Intelligence Summaries are contained in F.S. Regs., Part II. and the Staff Manual respectively. Title Pages will be prepared in manuscript.

Place	Date	Hour	Summary of Events and Information	Remarks and references to Appendices
Solingen	1/6/19		Church Parade.	
	2/6/19		Training as per programme.	
	3/6/19		Training as per programme.	
	4/6/19		Lecture by The Rev. McBane Ramsay M.A. B.D. on "The Past, Present, & Future of British-American Friendship."	
	5/6/19		Training as per programme. Baths for D. Coy. Back for Transport.	
	6/6/19		Training as per programme. Back for H.Q. Casuals.	
	7/6/19		Training as per programme. Sports held by A. Coy.	
	8/6/19		Church Parade.	
	9/6/19		D. Coy relieve B Coy in Outpost line. Training as per programme.	
	10/6/19		Training as per programme. Lecture by Mr Ralph Darlington F.R.G.S. on "Egypt, the Near East & the War."	
	11/6/19		Training as per programme. Baths for F. Coy.	

Army Form C. 2118.

WAR DIARY
or
INTELLIGENCE SUMMARY
(Erase heading not required.)

Instructions regarding War Diaries and Intelligence Summaries are contained in F. S. Regs., Part II. and the Staff Manual respectively. Title Pages will be prepared in manuscript.

Place	Date	Hour	Summary of Events and Information	Remarks and references to Appendices
Solingen 12/6/19	12/6/19		Bad. for Transport.	
	13/6/19		Training as per programme. Back to B'Coy. Barracks.	
	14/6/19		Training as per programme.	
	15/6/19		Do.	
	16/6/19		Church Parade.	
	17/6/19		Training as per programme.	
	18/6/19		Do.	
	19/6/19		Back to B Coy. Training as per programme. Back for Transport.	
	20/6/19		A. & D. boys relieved in Outpost line by 5/c. 153rd Bn. Gordon Highlanders. Back for H.Q. Coy. Barracks.	
	21/6/19		Battalion move to troubled area.	
	22/6/19		Church Parade.	
	23/6/19		Training as per programme.	
	24/6/19		Do.	
	25/6/19		Change of billeting H.Q. A. & D. Coys. Training as per programme. Do.	
	26/6/19		Change of billeting. Transport & B. Coy.	

Army Form C. 2118.

WAR DIARY
or
INTELLIGENCE SUMMARY
(Erase heading not required.)

Instructions regarding War Diaries and Intelligence Summaries are contained in F. S. Regs., Part II. and the Staff Manual respectively. Title Pages will be prepared in manuscript.

Place	Date	Hour	Summary of Events and Information	Remarks and references to Appendices
Solesmes	27/6/19		Inspection of Transport & Competition Training as per programme.	
	28/6/19		Peace Signed	
	29/6/19		Church Parade	
	30/6/19		Training as per programme	

Telegrams RMS
Conv S/Sgt H.M.

Rob Baird
Lieut

WAR DIARY.

51st BN. THE HIGHLAND LIGHT INFANTRY.

MONTH OF SEPTEMBER 1919.

                    Lieut. Col.
Commanding 51st Bn. The High. L. I.

Army Form C. 2118.

WAR DIARY
~~INTELLIGENCE SUMMARY~~

(Erase heading not required.)

Instructions regarding War Diaries and Intelligence Summaries are contained in F. S. Regs., Part II. and the Staff Manual respectively. Title Pages will be prepared in manuscript.

Place	Date	Hour	Summary of Events and Information	Remarks and references to Appendices
Stommeln	1-9-19		Training as per programme.	
	2-9-19		Baths for "D" Coy. Educational training as per programme.	
	3-9-19		Baths for HQ Coy.	
	4-9-19		Baths for Transport and Casuals. Battalion Route March	
	5-9-19		Baths for "A" Coy.	
	6-9-19		Training as per programme.	
	7-9-19		Church Parade	
	8-9-19		Baths for "C" Coy.	
	9-9-19		Training as per programme. Baths for "D" Coy.	
	10-9-19		Lecture by The Hon. Crawford Vaughan on "America and Britain"	
	11-9-19		Battalion Route March.	
	12-9-19		Training as per programme. Baths for "A" Coy.	
	13-9-19		Training as per programme. Baths for "B" Coy.	
	14-9-19		Church Parade.	
	15-9-19		Baths for "C" Coy. Training as per programme.	
	16-9-19		Baths for "D" Coy. do	
	17-9-19		Baths for HQ Coy. do	
	18-9-19		Battalion Route March. (Baths for Transport and Casuals. 19/6/19)	
	20-9-19		Training as per programme. Baths for "B" Coy.	
	21-9-19		Church Parade.	
	22-9-19		Training as per programme. Baths for "C" Coy.	
	23-9-19		Battalion Singing Practice. Baths for "D" Coy.	
	24-9-19		Training as per programme. Baths for HQ Coy.	
	25-9-19		Training as per programme. Baths for Transport and Casuals.	
	26-9-19		do	
Bedburg	27-9-19		Battalion Move to Bedburg.	
"	28-9-19		Coys. at disposal of Coy. Commanders.	
"	29-9-19		do	
	30-9-19		Training as per programme.	

WAR DIARY.

51st. BN. The HIGHLAND LIGHT INFANTRY.

FOR MONTH OF AUGUST. 1919.

Lt. Col.

Commanding 51st. Bn. High. L. I.

Army Form C. 2118.

WAR DIARY
or
INTELLIGENCE SUMMARY

(Erase heading not required.)

Instructions regarding War Diaries and Intelligence Summaries are contained in F. S. Regs., Part II. and the Staff Manual respectively. Title Pages will be prepared in manuscript.

Place	Date	Hour	Summary of Events and Information	Remarks and references to Appendices
Worringen	1-8-19		Training as per programme.	
"	2-8-19		do. do.	
	3-8-19		Church Parade.	
	4-8-19		Bank Holiday observed.	
	5-8-19		Training and Education as per programme.	
	6-8-19		do.	
	7-8-19		Lecture by Professor W. MacDougall F.R.S. B.Sc. "Heredity and the Future of the British Race"	
	8-8-19		Training and Education as per programme.	
	9-8-19		Battalion move from Worringen Area to Stommeln Area.	
Stommeln	10-8-19		Baths for "B" Company.	
	11-8-19		Training as per programme.	
	12-8-19		Church Parade.	
	13-8-19		Training as per programme.	
	14-8-19		Baths for "D" Coy.	
	15-8-19		Training and Education as per programme.	
	16-8-19		Baths for Transport and Casuals.	
	17-8-19		Battalion War Savings Association commenced.	
	18-8-19		Baths for "A" Coy.	
	19-8-19		Training as per programme.	
	20-8-19		Church Parade	
	21-8-19		Training and Education as per programme.	
	22-8-19		Baths for H.Q. Company.	
	23-8-19		Baths for Transport and Casuals.	
	24-8-19		Training and Education as per programme.	
	25-8-19		Battalion Route March.	
			Baths for "B" Company.	
			Baths for "C" Company.	
	26-8-19		Church Parade.	
			Brigade Athletic Championship won by 51st Bn. High. L.I.	
			Baths for "D" Company.	

Army Form C. 2118.

WAR DIARY
or
INTELLIGENCE SUMMARY
(Erase heading not required.)

Instructions regarding War Diaries and Intelligence Summaries are contained in F. S. Regs., Part II. and the Staff Manual respectively. Title Pages will be prepared in manuscript.

Place	Date	Hour	Summary of Events and Information	Remarks and references to Appendices
Stommeln	27-8-19		Baths for H.Q. Company.	
	28-8-19		Battalion Route March.	
	29-8-19		Battalion Cinema commenced.	
	30-8-19		Baths for "B" Company.	
	31-8-19		Church Parade.	

WAR DIARY.

51st BN. THE HIGHLAND LIGHT INFANTRY.

MONTH OF SEPTEMBER 1919.

Elsgrave
                Lieut. Col.
Commanding 51st Bn. The High. L. I.

Army Form C.2118.

WAR DIARY
or
INTELLIGENCE SUMMARY
(Erase heading not required.)

Instructions regarding War Diaries and Intelligence Summaries are contained in F.S. Regs., Part II. and the Staff Manual respectively. Title Pages will be prepared in manuscript.

Place	Date	Hour	Summary of Events and Information	Remarks and references to Appendices
Stommeln	1-9-19		Training as per programme.	
	2-9-19		Baths for "D" Coy. Educational training as per programme.	
	3-9-19		Baths for HQ Coy.	
	4-9-19		Baths for Transport and Casuals. Battalion Route March	
	5-9-19		Baths for "A" Coy.	
	6-9-19		Training as per programme.	
	7-9-19		Church Parade	
	8-9-19		Baths for "C" Coy.	
	9-9-19		Training as per programme. Baths for "D" Coy.	
	10-9-19		Lecture by The Hon. Crawford Vaughan on "America and Britain"	
	11-9-19		Battalion Route March.	
	12-9-19		Training as per programme. Baths for "A" Coy.	
	13-9-19		Training as per programme. Baths for "B" Coy.	
	14-9-19		Church Parade.	
	15-9-19		Baths for "C" Coy. Training as per programme.	
	16-9-19		Baths for "D" Coy. do do	
	17-9-19		Baths for HQ Coy. do do	
	18-9-19		Battalion Route March.(Baths for Transport and Casuals.	(19/9/1919)
	19-9-19		Training as per programme. Baths for "B" Coy.	
	20-9-19		Church Parade.	
	21-9-19		Training as per programme. Baths for "C" Coy.	
	22-9-19		Battalion Singing Practice. Baths for "D" Coy.	
	23-9-19		Training as per programme. Baths for HQ Coy.	
	24-9-19		Training as per programme. Baths for Transport and Casuals.	
	25-9-19		do do	
	26-9-19		Battalion Move to Bedburg.	
Bedburg	27-9-19		Coys. at disposal of Coy. Commanders.	
"	28-9-19		do	
"	29-9-19		do	
"	30-9-19		Training as per programme.	

www.ingramcontent.com/pod-product-compliance
Lightning Source LLC
Chambersburg PA
CBHW081509160426
43193CB00014B/2625